Duke 'n' Matt

Rescue Road Warriors

Written by Rhonda Paglia
Content and Photos contributed by Matt Pi
Published by Angels Landing

A Grammy Pags Story

Written by: Rhonda Paglia, a Grammy Pags Story
Content and Photographs contributed by: Matt "Pi" Piglowski
Edited by: Matt Pi and Jo Spring
Cover and Interior Design by: Rhonda Paglia

Books available from:
www.amazon.com
www.createspace.com

LCRN: pending
ISBN-13: 978-1500292607
ISBN-10: 1500292605

[1. animal rescue, 2. dog rescue, 3. pet rescue, 4. puppy mills
5. pet adoption, 6. Rescue Road Warriors]

First Edition
Published and printed in the United States of America
For information address: Angels Landing Publishing
347 Butterfly Lane, Hermitage, PA 16148
rhondapaglia@gmail.com

© August 2014

Dedicated to:

Duke 'n' Matt

and the rest of the
Rescue Road Warriors
Volunteers

Thanks for your work and for sharing your story!
Love, Grammy Pags

Rescue
Road
Warriors
www.RescueRoadWarriors.org

This is my book! I love being a Rescue Road Warrior!

This book also belongs to:

Josiah and Kaleb Stover AND
Naomi and Hannah Stover

Hi Friends, I hope you like my story. Be sure to check out the special "Learn More" and "Fun Stuff" pages in the back of the book. Thanks for loving and taking good care of your pets.

With love from your pal,

Duke

Rescue Road Warriors

I'm Duke and this is Matt. We are *Rescue Road Warriors!* I'm a red beagle. Matt's my best friend and the human part of our team.

We *volunteer* to help dogs get to places where they have a chance to be adopted by families who will love them.

Last night we got our *runsheet*. A runsheet is like a map. It tells us where to pick up our dogs, how many dogs we will pick up, and where we are to take them.

That means today is a rescue day! I can hardly wait! I love being a *Rescue Road Warrior*!

We helped rescue Austin. Look how happy he is!

Matt and I have special jobs as *Rescue Road Warriors.* First, Matt signs us up for the *transport.* We're like a taxi service for the dogs we rescue. We call them our *passengers.*

I'm ready to go!

Matt's other job is to drive our Beaglemobile on our *run.* It's called the Beaglemobile because we mostly pick up and rescue beagles.

Matt says my jobs are the most important ones. I'm the official greeter, host, and mascot. I help our rescue dogs get comfortable.

Matt is with another dog named Duke.

I'm not showing off or anything, but most dogs and people like me. Matt is the bushy-haired scraggy member of our team. I'm the handsome, friendly face that everyone loves.

We *Rescue Road Warriors* carry paperwork, food, treats, medication, and sometimes new toys for our dogs. We try to make them feel safe, protected, and loved.

3

Today, our runsheet tells us to meet our dogs in Youngstown, Ohio. This is our first *destination*. Our job is to drive them to their next destination, Milesburg, Pennsylvania.

When we pull the Beaglemobile into Youngstown, my heart beats really fast! Our passengers, Patches, Lily, Harley, and Eden, will be here soon.

Here is Matt
with Patches and Lily.

Many other *Rescue Road Warriors* are arriving too. Most of the *Warriors* at our stop are from Ohio or Pennsylvania. It takes many *Warriors* to help rescue and transport the dogs!

Our runsheet says that Eden and Lily came all the way from Missouri. Harley and Patches are from Indiana. I like our new passengers!

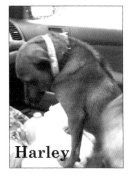

Most of the dogs we meet are rescued from temporary shelters or *puppy mills*. Some are from places where they were abused or abandoned. We *Warriors* are happy the dogs are safe with us. Now we can help get them closer to their new homes, their adoptive families, or to special rescue facilities.

4

This is Lily with me and Matt.
She came all the way
from Missouri.

Matt gets us all packed up, then it's time to leave. Here we come, Milesburg! It will take us about three hours to get there.

Sometimes our destinations are close to our home base, about 45 miles away. Our longest run was 650 miles. We drove all the way from St. Louis, MO to Erie, PA.

Where our journey takes us depends on where our rescue dogs are and where they need to go. Matt and I have driven lots of miles and, so far, we've transported more than 150 dogs!

Patches, Lily, Harley, and Eden are happy to see us.

But every once in a while, we have rescue dogs that are very scared!

They shiver and shake. Sometimes they are weak and unsteady on their paws.

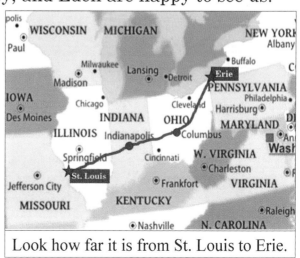

Look how far it is from St. Louis to Erie.

Petey

Destiny

Honey

Sometimes our dogs are so nervous, they don't want to come with us. Since I'm the official greeter, I use my best friendly manners to help our passengers get comfortable. I let them pick a toy or a special treat. That's being friendly AND polite!

Sometimes I snuggle with them until I feel their heartbeats slow down. I know how they feel. I needed rescuing before I met Matt. I was scared too.

I like getting to be one of our passengers' first new friends. Today, Patches, Lily, Harley, and Eden are doing great. They are happy AND calm.

As we travel to Milesburg, our new friends told me they feel safe and in good hands with me and Matt.

One time we transported Louie and his sister, Lucy.

I let them sit in the front seat with Matt.

6

I like to tell our passengers stories about the new friends they will make and the new family that may be waiting to love them. Our passengers also like to hear the story about my special friend, Moose.

Moose was a puppy when he and his sisters were rescued. They came from Missouri and were transported all the way to New Jersey. Matt and I helped Moose get to his new home. Moose's job was to be a therapy dog for a little girl who was sick.

The girl hadn't talked in over a year, but the first time she saw a picture of Moose, she said her first word. Guess what the word was? It was . . . "MOOSE!" That's how Moose got his name. Moose loves his new home, his new family, and especially the little girl. Moose has been a huge help, and the little girl has improved! She's talking a lot more and Moose is never lonely!

Here are Matt and Moose.

I told Patches, Lily, Harley, and Eden that I'm glad they've had all of their shots and that they are in good health. I'm also glad they've had a bath.

Winston

I told them that sometimes we transport dogs that have been hurt or injured. Some haven't had a bath in a REALLY long time. They stink a little bit.

Others dogs we've transported are so thin that their skin is wrinkling and saggy. We can see their bones through their skin. These dogs are *malnourished*. They haven't had enough clean water or healthy food.

I told them that we've driven dogs that are so scared, they are *flight risks*. That means they might run away. We watch these passengers very carefully and keep them close to us. We don't ever want to lose a dog. If they run away, they could get lost, hurt, or even die. We *Rescue Road Warriors* don't want any of our dogs to ever be in danger.

Today our friends are quiet. Harley is so content, he took a nap. He slept almost all of the way to Milesburg.

Sleepy Harley

8

Finally, we arrive in Milesburg. Patches, Lily, sleepy Harley, and Eden were great travelers. As we pull into our meeting place, the next group of *Rescue Road Warriors* is there. They will take our new friends on the next *leg* of their journey!

Lily is the closest to her new home. She's going to North Wales, PA. Patches, Harley, and Eden still have a long way to go. They are traveling all the way to Maine.

I'm so glad our rescue dogs will be going to families or safe places where people will love and care for them.

Good luck, my new friends!

Lily & Eden

Patches

Harley

Matt and I agree. The hardest part of this work is handing over the dogs we pick up. Matt told me that if I wasn't so jealous, he'd probably own lots of dogs. I'm happy we help deliver our rescue dogs to other families. That way, I get Matt all to myself!

Me and Matt,
my pal and best friend

Duke 'n' Matt
Rescue Road Warriors!
It's our job . . .
and we love it!
Love, Duke

Duke's REAL paw print!

My Story

Matt adopted me on May 1, 2009 through *Club Pet Adoption* in Transfer, PA. Just thinking about that day makes me so happy.

Matt said I was one of 52 beagles up for adoption. He said his biggest problem was trying to figure out which dog to pick!

Well, I have news for Matt! He didn't pick me . . . I picked him!

Matt and I are best buddies. We are a family.

Sometimes my heart floods over so much, I just have to jump up and give him big slobbery kisses, but he loves them!

Matt takes really good care of me. I always have plenty to eat and sometimes he gives me great treats. Greenies are my favorites.

Matt and I like to go for long walks. The park is my favorite place to go. I get to see all the different animals, like squirrels, rabbits, chipmunks, and of course, other dogs. I also get to sniff, sniff, sniff. Sniffing is another one of my favorite things to do.

We like to walk about three miles every day. By the time we are done, I've given Matt plenty of exercise.

We have a nice big yard where we like to play. I love to wrestle with Matt in the grass.

Did you know we've had passengers that have never walked on grass? That's because they have never, ever, been out of their cages or crates! I would not like that!

Matt needed a break, so I'm waiting on the bench.

Matt and I have met some dogs that haven't been petted or loved either. I can hardly believe it! I love to be petted and scratched behind my ears.

I have a nice, soft, cozy bed to sleep in and my house is so comfortable. I've got plenty of room to walk around and check things out.

I'm so lucky that my home is with Matt!

I love to play in the grass. 12

More About Our Rescue Dogs

Matt and I and the other *Warriors* have helped dogs from *puppy mills*. A puppy mill is a place where female dogs live and give birth to lots of puppies. Having babies is their only job. It's very hard on the mommy dogs to have so many puppies. Matt told me that *puppy mill breeders* can make a lot of money from the dogs that are born there.

Most often, dogs at puppy mills live in small cages. Sometimes many dogs live in the same cage. Some of our rescue dogs used to live in spaces that were so small, they couldn't even turn around.

Matt and I also help rescue dogs called *breeder releases*. These are dogs that breeders can't keep anymore.

The breeder will release the dogs into the care of the *Rescue Road Warriors* and we help get them to their new homes.

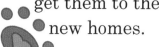

Lupita

13

Seal

Kodiak

Roo

Sometimes we pick up dogs that are well cared for, but because there are already too many dogs in one place, there just isn't enough space for everyone.

We've also helped rescue dogs when their owners are too sick to care for them. Sometimes people move into apartments where no pets are allowed. We pick up those dogs and help transport them to new homes too!

This is the *Toy Story Crew*:
Andy, Buzz, Jessie, Molly, Rex, Sarge, Trixie, and Woody.

Matt and I volunteer mainly with *Rescue Road Warriors*, but we also help other organizations, like *Club Pet Adoption*, *Open Arms Pound Rescue*, and *Ontario Bloodhound Rescue*. *These and other organizations and their websites are listed on page 29.*

This is me and Matt with another one of our rescue dogs, Moses, and our friend, Chris.

Thank you for adopting me, Matt! I love you!

More of Duke's Story
by Matt Pi

I adopted Duke from *Club Pet Adoption* on May 1, 2009, so we recently had our 5-year anniversary. He had just turned 4 when I adopted him, and on April 16 of this year [2014] he turned 9.

From what I understand, CEO Dianna Estman of *Club Pet*, at the time, would buy entire *litters* of beagle pups from a local "breeder" so the dogs would not have to suffer with him or with the people who would buy from him. Duke was part of one of these litters.

Duke, and his sister Daisy, were adopted out together as puppies, but later brought back to *Club Pet* because the family lost their business and could no longer afford to take care of them.

Daisy was adopted right back out. She lives in New Castle, PA, but Duke was stuck in the shelter for TWO YEARS before I came along. I found this to be unbelievable because Duke is such a great dog.

I like to think that he was waiting for me. As it says in the story, there were 52 beagles up for adoption the day I met Duke, so my biggest problem was picking one. Duke made the process easier by picking me.

Before Getting a Pet, Please Consider Pet Adoption
By Duke

I'm lucky! I was adopted and Matt takes really good care of me! Matt says that pet neglect, abuse, overpopulation, and abandonment are big problems in the world today. We *Rescue Road Warriors* do what we can to help solve these problems. YOU can too!

A Few Do's and Don'ts from Duke

DO ~

1. DO make sure you really want a pet. Research and choose a pet that is right for your family.
2. DO make sure your pet fits your living space and lifestyle. REMEMBER - a pet is just like YOU - an important member of your family.
3. DO give your pet: healthy food to eat, clean water, a comfortable bed, lots of exercise, love, and attention.
4. DO make sure your pet has a yearly checkup with a veterinarian and is current on their shots.
5. DO consider pet adoption. Check out the local animal shelters and pet rescue groups.

DON'T ~

1. DON'T buy a pet just because it's cute. Take your time! Research. Make sure your needs match your pet's needs.

Rose

2. DON'T get a pet if you can't give it a lot of your time and attention.
3. DON'T get a pet if you can't afford to take good care of all its needs.
4. DON'T abuse or neglect your pet. Most pets, especially dogs, give unconditional love. Be patient, especially if you get a puppy.
5. DON'T ever leave your pet in a hot car.

Duke Says,

"Here's more to learn and

some fun stuff to do!"

18

Duke's Definitions

Here are some special words from
my story and what they mean.

Canine: Another name for dog.

Breeder: A person who mates dogs to produce
puppies with special qualities and characteristics.
Some breeders produce dogs to sell and make money.

Breeder - PROFESSIONAL: These breeders understand the science of
"genetics" or "dog genes." [See "Genes" below.] They breed strong, healthy
dogs and don't let the mother dog have any more litters than necessary. Their
dogs get healthy food, are up-to-date on their shots, and receive lots of
attention. They treat their dogs with love and kindness and give them plenty of
exercise and training. They don't often sell their puppies, but when they do,
they choose homes for the puppies very carefully.

Breeder - PUPPY MILL: A puppy mill breeder is a business person. They
have dogs that produce a lot of puppies very quickly. Sometimes these breeders
don't know how to breed their dogs properly. Often, they don't follow the laws
and don't take good care of their dogs. Puppy mill breeders can make a lot of
money selling these puppies.

Breeder Releases: Dogs that breeders don't want or can't take care of
anymore.

Destination: The place where we pick up or drop off a rescue dog.
Sometimes we get to take rescue dogs to their "final" destination, their new
families.

Flight risk: Dogs that are so scared, they might try to run away.

Genes: Genes are tiny cells in our bodies that determine if we will have brown
or blonde hair, blue or brown eyes. Genes determine if we will be tall or short,
an athlete or an artist. Genes in dogs decide a dog's color, their size, and what
breed the dog will be. There are many kinds of dogs. I'm a beagle. I'm very
different from a Yorkshire terrier or a Great Dane or a tiny Chihuahua. Dogs,
and people too, are different because of their genes.

Leg: A part of a long-distance trip. Matt and I took Patches, Lily, Harley,
and Eden on three legs of their journey to help them get to their new
homes.

19

Little Henry

Litter: A litter is a group of puppies born at the same time from the same mother and father. The female / mom dog can have one, two or many more puppies in her litter.

Littermates: Animals from the same litter are called "littermates."

Malnourished: When an animal, plant, or human hasn't had enough healthy food to eat.

Passengers: These are what we call the dogs we rescue. Our passengers ride in our Beaglemobile.

Puppy Mill or Puppy Farm: This is a place where lots of puppies are born. Sometimes, there are so many puppies, the cages aren't very clean. Sometimes, these puppies don't get enough food and water. Sometimes, they don't get good care and get hurt or die. There are also "kitty mills" and other "animal mills" in the United States. These "mills" produce lots of animals that are often sold in pet stores, in newspapers, and on the Internet.

Rescue Road Warriors: These are volunteers, like me and Matt, from all over the United States. We pick up dogs that need to be rescued and deliver them to rescue facilities, foster homes, and adoptive families who are waiting for their new pet. There are over 900 *Rescue Road Warriors* on Facebook.

Run: Driving passengers from one place to another. Sometimes we may have more than one run a day. Other times, our runs may take us several days.

Runsheet: This is the paper that tells the *Rescue Road Warriors* where we are to go, what kind and how many dogs we are going to pick up, and where we are to take them.

Transport: To move from one place to another. Transport is part of the word *transportation.*

Volunteer: A volunteer is a person who helps others without getting paid. Examples would be people who help in hospitals, churches, and for emergency rescue, like volunteer fire fighters. Matt and I are *Rescue Road Warriors* volunteers. We volunteer to help deliver dogs to safe places.

I'm a happy *Rescue Road Warriors* volunteer! 20

FIND THE STATES: Duke and Matt have traveled to all 48 states shown below. *Rescue Road Warriors* have transported rescue dogs in and through the states listed on the right. Some rescue teams travel all the way to the Canadian border. Can you locate the states on the map?

__Connecticut __Massachusetts __Ohio
__Illinois __Missouri __Pennsylvania
__Indiana __New Hampshire __Wisconsin
__Maine __New Jersey
__Maryland __New York

Can you also find Canada?

NADA

MINNESOTA

MAINE

Montpelier ⊙Augusta
⊙

N.H.
VER. ⊙Concord

Minneapolis

WISCONSIN MICHIGAN

NEW YORK
Albany⊙ MASS.⊙Boston
⊙Providence

St. Paul

⊙
Milwaukee Lansing

•Buffalo

CONN. Hartford
⊙
•New York R.I.

Madison

⊙
•Detroit

PENNSYLVANIA N. JERSEY
Philadelphia • ⊙Trenton

IOWA

Chicago

Cleveland

Harrisburg⊙

Des Moines

⊙
INDIANA

Cleveland

DELAWARE
⊙Dover

ILLINOIS Indianapolis

OHIO

MARYLAND ⊙Annapolis

⊙Columbus

Springfield

Cincinnati

W. VIRGINIA

Washington D.C.

•St. Louis

⊙Charleston

⊙Richmond

ka ⊙

Jefferson City

⊙Frankfort

VIRGINIA

nsas City

KENTUCKY

MISSOURI

⊙Raleigh

na City

⊙Nashville

N. CAROLINA

TENNESSEE

Little Rock •Memphis

S. CAROLINA
⊙

OMA ARKANSAS

ALABAMA ⊙Atlanta

Columbia

MISSISSIPPI
⊙

GEORGIA

•Dallas

Montgomery

Jackson

Baton Rouge
⊙

⊙Tallahassee

Houston
•

•New Orleans

LOUISIANA

FLORIDA

Miami

22

Help Duke Match the Words & Definitions

____Breeder

____Breeder-PROFESSIONAL

____Breeder releases

____Flight risk

____Genes

____Litter

____Littermates

____Malnourished

____Passenger

____Puppy mill

____Rescue Road Warriors

____Runsheet

____Transport

____Volunteer

A. Breeders who understand the science of "dog genes."

B. Volunteers who pick up and deliver dogs to rescue facilities, foster homes, and families.

C. Someone who rides in a car like the Beaglemobile.

D. Tiny cells in our bodies that determine characteristics.

E. A person who mates a mother and father dog to produce puppies.

F. When an animal, plant, or human hasn't had enough food or healthy food to eat.

G. A group of puppies born at the same time from the same mom and dad.

H. A place where lots of puppies are born.

I. Someone who helps others without getting paid.

J. Dogs that breeders don't want or can't take care of anymore.

K. This information tells *Rescue Road Warriors* about the dogs they will pick up and where they are to take them.

L. To move something from one place to another.

M. Animals born in the same litter.

N. A dog that might run away.

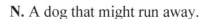

Look Back in the Story

1. What is the name of the car that Duke and Matt use to pick up the rescue dogs?

   _____

2. About how many *Rescue Road Warriors* are there in the United States? _____

3. Matt says Duke has important jobs when they go on a rescue run. What are Duke's jobs? _____,

   _____, _____.

4. _____ are Duke's favorite treats.

5. Duke loves to go to the _____ for his walks. He and Matt walk about _____ miles a day.

6. _____ is the name of the rescue dog that helped a little girl talk again. Where was he born? _____

7. Duke 'n' Matt transported _____, _____,

   _____, and _____, from Youngstown, OH to Milesburg, PA.

8. Who slept most of the way to Milesburg? _____

9. Duke says, "Before getting a pet, please consider pet _____."

10. "Can you find my REAL paw print in this book?" asks Duke.

Check your answers on Duke's Answer Page!

24

Do you remember
any of Duke's Do's and Don'ts?

Draw a picture and show Duke what YOU would do
to take good care of your pet!

Do you want to see your picture on Grammy's website?
E-mail your picture to: grammypags1@gmail.com

Duke's Answer Page

Match the Words & Definitions

E - Breeder

A - Breeder-PROFESSIONAL

J - Breeder releases

N - Flight risk

D - Genes

G - Litter

M - Littermates

F - Malnourished

C - Passenger

H - Puppy mill

B - Rescue Road Warriors

K - Runsheet

L - Transport

I - Volunteer

Look Back in the Story

1. Beaglemobile
2. 900
3. Greeter, host, mascot
4. Greenies
5. Park, 3
6. Moose, Missouri
7. Patches, Lily, Harley, Eden
8. Harley
9. Adoption
10. My REAL paw print is on page 10.

Duke and Moses

More about *Rescue Road Warriors* from Founder Kerin Hanson

Kerin Hanson

I have had a life-long love for animals. I tried to become involved in other areas of rescue and have always adopted from shelters, but it wasn't until I was introduced to volunteer rescue transports that animal rescue became the centerpiece of my life. I wanted to help and I wanted to help on a grand scale.

In 2009, I founded an organization called the *Rescue Road Warriors* to help save the lives of neglected, abused and abandoned animals by moving them to other areas of the country that allowed more opportunity for adoption. *Rescue Road Warriors* is an all-volunteer transport organization, comprised of several hundred compassionate citizens who spend a few hours per month providing transport for rescue animals. The transports are set up as a relay, leaving Missouri and traveling as far northeast as Maine and to the Canadian border.

Over the course of the past five years, so many wonderful things have happened in our *Rescue Road Warrior* community. We have not only built a community that has supported saving the lives of over 8,000 rescue animals (including dogs, cats, three turtles, two goats, and a miniature horse), we are a rescue family that has established a gas fund to assist our drivers, and have networked locally to support those in our community, beyond rescue transport. We are a family with a shared mission to give voice to the voiceless. Each transport is a blessing and each life saved is a gift.

If you are interested in learning more about our rescue community, please don't hesitate to contact us at:
information@rescueroadwarriors.org.

More about *Rescue Road Warrior* Matt Pi

Jonah and Matt

At his day job, **Matthew S. Piglowski,** also known as "Matt Pi," works as a mathematician and author at Larson Texts, Inc., Erie, PA. Prior to this, he taught mathematics and engineering technology at Kent State University, Ashtabula, OH and Edinboro University of Pennsylvania, Edinboro, PA and has held several engineering positions.

He has a Bachelors degree in Electrical Engineering from Gannon University, Erie, PA, and a Masters degree in Electric Power Engineering from Rensselaer Polytechnic Institute, Troy, NY.

He enjoys travel, music, working out, volunteering, and spending time with Duke. Their first transport was on July 21, 2012, where they drove two puppies, Rosie and Sophie, across a portion of New York state.

We're at the end of our story.
The rescue dogs are happy, the new families are happy, and Duke 'n' Matt and the rest of the *Rescue Road Warriors* have put in another good day!

Visit Duke 'n' Matt on Facebook: www.facebook.com/matt.pi.77

For more information about adopting and / or fostering a rescue dog, here's a partial list:

- Rescue Road Warriors: www.rescueroadwarriors.org

- Club Pet Adoption, Transfer, PA: www.clubpetadopt.com

◆ ◆ ◆ ◆ ◆ ◆

- A.N.A. Shelter (Association for Needy and Neglected Animals), Erie, **PA**: www.theannashelter.com

- Because You Care, Inc., McKean, PA: www.becauseyoucare.org

- Droopy Basset Hound Rescue of Western PA: www.droopybassetrescue.com

- **Humane Society of Northwestern Pennsylvania:** www.humanesocietyofnwpa.com

- **Humane Society of the US:** www.humanesociety.org

- **HuskyN Lab Rescue**: www.huskynlabrescue.org

- **Mercy Fund Animal Rescue, Inc., Marion, NC:** www.mercyanimalrescue.rescueme.org

- **Ontario Bloodhound Rescue:** www.bloodhoundrescue.ca

- **Open Arms Pound Rescue:** www.openarmspoundrescue.com

Check Online - Pet Events & Fundraisers

- A.N.A. Shelter ~ Pup Crawl
- **Because You Care ~ Walk for Small Animals**
- **Droopy Basset Hound Rescue ~ Slobberfest**
- **DukeFest Dog Walk**
- **Kori's Critters ~ Benefit in Support of Animal Rescue**

To make a tax deductible contribution, go to:

www.rescueroadwarriors.org

and click on the Donate button.

A significant portion
of the profit from this book
benefits Rescue Road Warriors
and their work.

Fresno

Yogi

Spike

Ike

Ranger

Pork
Chop &
Evelyn

Duke

Sam

Thank you
for your
support!

Adelaide

Boo

Duke 'n' Matt

Emily

Sherlock

Lila

Shirley

Miley

Earthy & Matt

32

Watch for future details about the

*Catherine Violet Hubbard
Animal Sanctuary.*

Catherine was a 6-year-old victim of the
Sandy Hook Elementary School tragedy.
The *Catherine Violet Hubbard Animal
Sanctuary* expects to open in 2016.
It is being built to honor Catherine
and her love for all animals.

FOR INFORMATION:
cvhfoundation.org/animalsanctuary

www.facebook.com/
CatherineVioletHubbardAnimalSanctuary

33

Rhonda Paglia is a retired elementary teacher from Pennsylvania. She and her husband, Tony, have three grown children, five grandchildren, and one little lovable Yorkie-poo named Bella (who did not come from a puppy mill).

Rhonda, known as "Grammy Pags," loves writing stories for her grandchildren and other kids. To date, **Duke 'n' Matt, Rescue Road Warriors** is her fifth children's book to be released to the public.

Grammy Rhonda says, "I hope this book will help readers learn about the benefits of pet adoption. There is so much to think about and to consider before bringing a pet into your home."

Other stories by "Grammy Pags"

The Little Lambs and the Very Special Mission (dedicated to the children and teachers of Sandy Hook), written by Rhonda Paglia and co-illustrated Rhonda Paglia and Taylor Galaska.

Doonsey's Beach Adventure, the Great Rescue and *Doonsey's Beach Adventure, the Great Rescue Coloring and Activity Book* written and illustrated by Rhonda Paglia.

Three Little Gnomes and a Boy Named Orion written by Rhonda Paglia and illustrated by Ratna Kusuma Halim.

Visit Grammy Pags' author page on Amazon:
www.amazon.com/-/e/B00G5X3WO2

If you like this story,
please post a review
on www.amazon.com.

You can visit or contact Rhonda "Grammy Pags" at:

Facebook: www.facebook.com/grammypagsstories

Website: www.rhondapagliaauthor.com

Amazon: www.amazon.com/-/e/B00G5X3WO2

Blog: www.rhondapaglia.blogspot.com

Twitter: www.twitter.com/grammypags1

Grammy's newsletter: grammypags1@gmail.com

Made in the USA
Lexington, KY
09 August 2014